buggy-go-round

buggy-go-round

by E. and R.S. Radlauer

illustrated with photographs by the authors

Franklin Watts, Inc., 845 Third Avenue, New York, New York 10022

SBN 531-01991-8. Copyright © 1971 by E. and R. S. Radlauer
Library of Congress Catalog Card Number: 76-151888. Printed in the United States of America

4   5

A Buggy-Go-Round. That's what I call our sport, Roundy Buggy Racing. Whatever they call it, it's a great sport. I know because I've gone around the track a lot of times. Our track isn't really round like the name says. But the **buggies** go round and round on the closed **circuit.**

The track is a closed dirt circuit with **straightaways,** turns, jumps, bumps, and a waterhole.

Roundy Buggies are set up for quick **acceleration,** quick braking, and quick steering. Everything quick. Everything happens quick on the roundy circuit. If a driver doesn't have quick acceleration he only gets in the way of the others. That can mean trouble.

4

There's plenty of action on the buggy track. The big action is in the turns and over the jumps.

A lot of the roundy buggy action happens in the turns. If a driver comes off the straightaway too fast, he could flip his buggy or **loop** it in the turn. Some drivers get up to 40 miles an hour on the straightaway. Then they have to do some fancy braking before they hit the turn.

But a looped buggy isn't all that bad. Everybody loops his buggy now and then. We say it's a pretty funny feeling, sitting there while the race goes on around you. A driver in a looped buggy tries to get back in the running. He wants back in the race and he doesn't want people to see how red his face is because he looped in the turn!

Some people bring their buggies to the track on a trailer. Others load them in a truck or tow them behind a car. It doesn't matter how a guy gets his buggy to the track as long as he gets there.

The early people wait in line to **sign up** for racing. The waiting around isn't bad because there's lots of talk about engines, buggies, and racing. Before the races start, everyone seems to know the special magic it takes to win. Or they talk about the special bad luck that made them lose the last race day.

A few people use the time before the races to work on their buggies. I guess that could be one kind of magic that helps people win.

A driver who loops his buggy ends up face to face with some of the other drivers. Is that a good way to meet friends?

Use a trailer, use a truck, use a towrope. Just be sure to get to the Buggy-Go-Round.

I guess every kind of racing has **inspectors** and inspection. A friend of mine who runs the 100-yard dash in track meets says there's even a doctor to inspect him before the race.

We don't have doctors for the Roundy Buggy inspection. We have inspectors who know what to look for to be sure a buggy is safe. They check the **fire wall** between the driver and the engine. They check to make sure the battery is bolted down tight. When a driver takes his buggy over a jump, he doesn't want the battery to fly out.

After inspection, everyone heads for the **pits** to unload the buggy and get ready for racing. Sometimes it's a one-man team that unloads. Then there are some big teams that have an owner, mechanics, a **pit crew** boss, and driver. That's what I think is so great about Roundy Buggy racing. Everyone is welcome.

But getting ready is the same with a one-man crew or a big team. The buggy has to be unloaded, **fueled up,** and checked over.

I know some buggy drivers who don't want help. Each one is so fussy about his machine he won't let *anyone* touch it.

Inspectors check everything but the driver's tonsils. They'd even check the driver's tonsils if he had any.

Slow and straight is the rule for unloading a buggy from a trailer. No need for the engine, just ride the brakes.

As soon as the **officials** give the word that the track is open, everyone goes out to practice. The practice helps drivers get the feel of the track.

By going around the track a lot of times, drivers get to know how fast to take a turn and how much speed to use over a jump.

A driver doesn't *have* to go **airborne** after a jump, but if he gets up any speed at all, his buggy just naturally lifts all four right off the top of the jump. Then he just naturally has to come down. Everyone agrees that going up is easy. It's coming down that's hard.

10

The faster a buggy is going over a jump, the higher it goes. Front wheels straight during a jump is the rule.

Every so often the **water truck** has to make its run. That water truck has one big job. With a dry track there's too much dust. But the water truck driver has to be careful, because a track that is too wet is too slippery. A buggy can't get up any speed on a slippery track.

Some tracks have a special dirt called **clay.** Dirt that holds water makes a good hard track like damp clay.

If it's a hot day, the water truck has to make lots of runs. A water truck never won a **trophy,** got airborne on a jump, or set any track records. But without it, none of the drivers would win trophies or set records. There wouldn't be any races!

Most Roundy Buggies use **air-cooled** engines. The four **cylinder VW** engine is very popular, but a few like the six cylinder **Corvair** engine. Whichever kind a buggy has, it's not like it was when it powered a family car. These engines have had a lot done to them to make them more powerful.

For one thing, there are what we call 180 degree **exhaust headers.** The 180 degree shape and length make one cylinder help pull the **exhaust gas** out of another.

Someone once asked me, "What good is all that spaghetti looking exhaust stuff?" I told him that spaghetti looking stuff might add as much as 10 **horsepower** to an engine.

The water truck driver has to go at the right speed to get the right amount of water on the track.

Special headers give more engine power. Strong bars protect the engine in case of bumping.

It's easy to tell a Corvair engine from a VW engine. On the Corvair the **fan and cooling shroud** lie down flat, like a table. On the VW the fan and cooling shroud stand up, right behind the driver's seat.

Which engine is better? I've sat up all night listening to guys argue about that. And when the arguing was over, I couldn't tell which guy was right.

Anyway, I always say an engine is only as good as the people who take care of it—right?

The VW engine is on the left, the Corvair on the right. Which is better? The one that wins is better!

Before the racing starts, each driver takes his **qualifying runs.** Then he goes into a racing **class** according to his **qualifying time** and his driving experience.

According to the rules, the new drivers go into a **novice** class. Drivers who have been racing a while and are pretty good go into the **expert** class.

A driver has to stay in the novice class until our club officials think his driving is good enough for the expert class. Some drivers make expert after just a few races. Then we have had drivers who never got out of the novice class.

The most important official on our Roundy track is the man called the **starter.** All the other officials watch him to know what is going on. He gives the **flag signals** that tell the drivers what to do. And the starter is the only official who can put someone off the track.

The flag signals in Roundy racing are like the flag signals in most other kinds of racing. **Green** means go. The **white** flag means there's one lap left in the race. The **red** flag is a signal to stop because of an accident. **Yellow** means to be careful, go slow, and no passing. When a driver gets the **black** flag, he knows there's something wrong with his machine or his driving!

Everyone knows what the **checkered** flag means.

To qualify, a driver makes a single fast lap. Then he goes into a class according to his qualifying time.

The starting-line official jumps with green flag to tell the drivers go! He's also jumping out of the way.

Our track has two main turns, but some drivers say the track feels like it's all turns. Of course that isn't true, because the track has jumps. Some drivers take the jump as if it was just a hill. They drive over it. Others get up more speed and go airborne.

To go airborne, a driver has to come into the jump pretty fast. Then going airborne and lifting all four off the ground takes care of itself. The driver has to take care to have his wheels straight when he comes down. If the front wheels are **cranked** over, the buggy's nose goes down and all the parts in the front end take a beating.

Going airborne looks easy. It is. It's coming down from being airborne that's hard!

When a buggy takes a jump, it's easy to see why it needs **four-wheel independent axles.** A straight-across, or **solid axle** wouldn't spring enough on this kind of track. With an independent axle, each wheel springs over the bumps and jumps. That helps the driver control his buggy.

The **suspension system,** or springs, on the axles are important, too. With a suspension that's too soft, an axle can **bottom,** hit the **chassis,** and break something. A suspension system that's too solid is no suspension at all. The stiffness of the suspension springs and buggy weight have to match each other. The heavier the buggy weight, the stronger the suspension springs have to be.

Faster and more expert drivers take the turns in what we call a **power slide.** They come up on a turn moving pretty fast, **rev** the engine to make the back wheels **break loose,** then crank the front wheels *away* from the turn. That sends the buggy into the slide.

In a power slide everything has to be done at the right time. If the rear wheels don't break loose, it's not a true power slide. And if the driver doesn't rev his engine and crank the front wheels at the right time, he'll loop his buggy or spin off the track.

A driver who can make good power slides doesn't have to slow down much going through a turn.

Like ouch! Having independent four wheel axles helps when coming down from a jump. Each independent axle takes up some of the shock.

Water truck or not, some drivers make dust when they do a power slide through a turn.

Maybe Roundy Dusty Racing would be a better name for the sport. Even with regular trips from our water truck, the track still gets dusty on a hot day. The heat from the sun, tires, and engines dries out the clay and then the dust flies.

Dust is bad stuff for engines and moving parts. That's why the buggies have special **air cleaners** on the **carbs.** That helps keep most of the dust out of the engine. Dust in an engine makes parts grind and wear out.

Some of our drivers wear their own air cleaners—masks made out of wet cloth.

One of the events in the Roundy Buggy Racing is called the **trophy dash.** We have the trophy dash right after qualifying is over. It's a special race for the five or six fastest qualifiers.

We give the winner of the trophy dash just that, a giant trophy and some money. The trophy dash makes a good race to watch and there's another reason for having it. That reason is to get all the drivers to do their best during qualifying.

Sometimes a driver tries to get a slow time during the qualifying so he can get in a slower class and have a better chance to win. We call that **sandbagging.** The trophy dash is supposed to keep drivers from sandbagging.

My day to get in the trophy dash is still coming.

The air cleaner is at the top of the bug frame.
The air goes to the carb through a big hose.

Is this what racing is all about? It's a big part
of it, anyway. But there's more.

The buggies on the Roundy track are pretty safe. That's because they are almost all **rollcage.** The bars of the rollcage have to be made of a special steel that doesn't bend or crack. The shape of the **rollbars** is important too, because the wrong shape can bend or crack.

The rollbar near the driver's arm is important. It's there to keep the driver's arm inside the buggy in case of a roll over.

A strong **safety harness** keeps the driver in place in case of an accident. Some men put pads on the harness. It's a good idea, because after a few races the harness makes a guy's shoulders pretty sore.

Some people come out and race **full-bodied** VW's. There isn't too much speed in a full-bodied VW or even one with part of a body, but they're fun to race, anyway. But since we race buggies in classes, everyone has a chance to win.

With a full-bodied VW, the **wheel wells** have to be cut and reshaped. If the wheel wells weren't reshaped, the big tires would scrape against the body and get torn up.

The full-bodied buggy is good for other kinds of racing, even those that run in the rain. We don't run Roundy races in the rain. The water truck gives all the rain we need!

The harness keeps the driver in place. The pads on the harness help keep the driver's skin in place!

Full-bodied buggies have chopped wheel wells. Without chopped wheel wells, tires get torn.

On some days we have a special show along with the races. Anyone who has ever seen motorcycle **sidehack** racing knows it's a special show.

The sidehack teams go over the same track as the buggies. The jumps, bumps, and turns give the teams a real workout.

The rider in the **sidecar** or sidehack has a real workout, too. He has to lean just right to keep the **rig** from tipping over or sliding off the track.

When the rider and his partner work together, they can get up some pretty good speeds. I asked one sidehack driver how it was, riding that thing. He said, "My partner and I gotta believe in each other."

I believed him!

*Three-wheel buggy? No, sidehack action. Some people call the driver the **pilot** and his passenger the **monkey.***

When the sidehack riders started over the jumps I didn't think any of them would go airborne. I was wrong. Some teams got up speed, went up the jump, and didn't lift all four, only three!

Buggy drivers have to be careful how they put the wheels down after a jump. Sidehack riders have to be even more careful when they lift all three. If the wrong wheel comes down first, there's no telling what the rig will do. So right after the jump, the driver and his partner lean back so the rear wheel comes down first, the side wheel next, and front wheel last. If the front wheel came down first, the whole rig could go into a spin.

After the sidehack riders finish, we run **heat races** for the buggies. There are no trophies in the heat races, just **points.** We give first place four points, three points for second, two for third place, and one point for finishing the race.

When the three heat races for each class are over, the drivers with the most points go in the **main event race.** The winners of the main event get the big trophies and the big money.

Our drivers like the trophies but they say they like the money even better. It costs money to build a buggy and keep it running. Think of those tires, engines, and broken parts that have to be replaced.

*Even sidehack rigs go airborne on the buggy
track. This team has good riding style.*

*When a racing class is this big, everyone better
watch out going through the turns.*

Sometimes things get a little crowded in the turns, especially right after the start of the race when all the buggies are packed together. There are no rules about buggies bumping together in a crowd. Sometimes drivers get bumped right off the track.

When that happens the driver tries to get back on the track and go on with the racing, if his buggy isn't broken.

With broken buggies most drivers drop out of the race, but a few have finished races with broken buggies.

Sometimes turns get so crowded that there's no place to go but off the track. Anyone know how to ride a telephone pole?

Inside one of the turns on the buggy track we have a small pond or lake. It's about two feet deep and ten feet across. All the drivers agree that it's not a very good place to go fishing—or driving.

Well, maybe none of the drivers go fishing in our pond but a few go bathing in it! They go bathing when they get bumped into the water or find themselves cutting off too much of the turn.

A trip into the lake is the end of the race for most buggies. But a few can come through the water without soaking their engines. After that it sure feels funny to be driving with boots that are full of water!

For people who really like water there are some buggy tracks that have a **water crossing.** It's part of the course. Everyone in the race makes a water crossing every lap.

Driving a course with a water crossing has plenty of special problems. There's the problem of soaking an engine. There's the problem of going too slow, losing power, and getting stalled in the water. It's not easy to start a stalled engine that's sitting "in the drink."

No matter how a driver makes the water crossing, he's going to get wet and so is his engine. That isn't too bad for the driver if it's a hot day. But who ever heard of a water-cooled—air-cooled engine? Only in buggy racing!

Someone taking a bath when it isn't even
Saturday night? Oh well, the buggy was dusty
and needed washing, anyway.

When a track has a water crossing, it's bathtime
if the drivers want it or not. Who's got the soap?

Most buggies can make the water crossing because the engine's **ignition system** has been **waterproofed.** Well, *almost* waterproofed. It's done by putting heavy grease on the ignition wires and parts. The grease keeps the water out. Well, it's *supposed* to keep the water out of the ignition system.

But the grease makes another problem. If any water does get into the ignition system, the grease does its job backward. It keeps the water in! I can tell you it's a mess, opening, cleaning, and drying up the ignition parts after the whole thing has been covered with grease, dirt, and water. Maybe that's why the guys say, "If you like clean, dry hands, stay out of buggy racing!"

Some guys take the water crossing with a driving style that's slow and easy. They hardly stir up a shower. Here's how their thinking goes: I'll put my buggy in low gear, keep up the engine power, look for the place where the water isn't deep, and come through with a dry engine. No shower for me!

This kind of driving doesn't make a big show, but at least it gives the driver a chance to finish the race. I guess that's a kind of driving skill, thinking out ways to stay in the running. But in thinking up ways to stay in the running, a guy should never forget about the other drivers. What will they do?

34

Grease on the ignition is supposed to keep the water out. A buggy with a wet ignition just doesn't run very well.

If a buggy has a plastic bucket seat, the driver gets to sit in a bucket full of water.

That's right! There's no telling what the other drivers will do. Some hit the water crossing going **wide open** and make a twenty-foot-wide water shower. Their thinking goes like this: I'll hit the water fast, with enough speed to carry me through so I don't have to slow and drop gears. Being in the water for a short time means less chance to soak the ignition. Then I'll come out of the water fast and have a chance to get ahead!

Well, that's *another* skill and driving style. It works sometimes. But what about the guy on the other side trying to "cool it" through the water crossing to stay dry? I guess he gets cooled in more ways than one.

Some drivers like a shower bath instead of a bath in a bucket. And the water isn't even warm!

On some tracks we run the **4x4,** or **four-wheel-drive,** classes. These are big machines that *can* give power to all four wheels when it's needed in rough country. In Roundy racing drivers don't use four-wheel drive, but there are plenty of places in the desert where it comes in handy.

The 4x4 class rules say that a buggy must have two men in each car during a race. That's because some of these rigs are used in 200 or 300 mile cross-country or desert races. It's not a good idea to go on a 200 mile desert race all alone.

These big buggies can really move. It's not any VW or Corvair engine that powers them. Most of them have giant **V-8** engines with as much as 400 horsepower.

Now you can see why I think buggy racing is such a great sport. It's my sport because it has jumps, turns, water, and lots of different kinds of machines. It gives a guy a chance to build up, run, and race a rig of his own.

Everyone in the Buggy-Go-Round races to win. And everyone knows that you have to come in first to win. It's coming in first that's the problem. It's a problem with a lot of little problems like how to jump, make a fast turn, take a water crossing, and have the feel of the track. The drivers say if a guy can get it all together in the right way, he has a good chance to win.

An airborne four-wheel-drive buggy comes down just a little hard! But they're built to take it.

The checkered flag is good news for drivers in first, second, or third place. It means a trophy or money.

One of these days I'll find out what it takes and how it is to come in a winner, because I'm building my buggy just the way I want it. I buy parts whenever I have the money and work on it whenever I have the time.

I've studied every driving style and machine in the sport. And I can tell you no one will know the track or have a better feel of it than I do, because ever since it opened, I've been the guy who drove the water truck. So when I show up with my buggy, everyone watch out! It's the end.

40

It's the end!

Glossary/Index

(Page number indicates where
the word first appears in the book)

43

Cooling shroud, p. 14	*See* **Fan and cooling shroud.**
Corvair, p. 12	An American car that is no longer built. The six-cylinder air-cooled engine is used in dirt buggies.
Cranked, p. 18	Steering wheels turned as far as they will go.
Cylinder, p. 12	The part of an engine where air and fuel are burned.
Exhaust gas, p. 12	The burned gas from an engine.
Exhaust headers, p. 12	Exhaust pipes.
Expert, p. 16	A person who has been racing a long time and drives very well.
Fan and cooling shroud, p. 14	Many air-cooled engines have a fan that blows air around them. A cover, or **shroud,** around the engine and fan makes the air move close to the engine.
Fire wall, p. 8	A metal wall between the driver and the engine.
Flag signals, p. 16	Signals used to tell drivers and other track workers what to do. They are: **black** — get off the track (usually one driver) **checkered** — end of race. First three to pass it are winners **green** — go **red** — all cars stop **white** — one more lap **yellow** — go slow, no passing
Four-wheel-drive, 4x4, p. 38	A car that has four driving wheels instead of the usual two.
Four-wheel independent axle, p. 20	*See* **Independent axle.**

44

45

Ruth and Ed Radlauer, authors of over fifty books for young people, are graduates of UCLA. They have worked as teachers, school administrators, reading specialists, and instructors in creative writing. Their works include books in the areas of science, language, social studies and, more recently, high-interest reading materials. Along with their three children, two horses, a dog, and an ancient cat, the Radlauers live in La Habra, California.

The books in the Sports Action series are *On the Drag Strip, Scramble Cycle, Horsing Around, Buggy-go-Round, On the Sand, Chopper Cycle, Salt Cycle, Motorcycle Mutt, Bonneville Cars, On the Water, Foolish Filly,* and *Racing on the Wind.*